Contents

D0489186

Collecting campaign medals

Although the granting of war medals can be traced back many hundreds of years, a regularised system of official awards began only after 1815 and the issuing of the Waterloo Medal. During the nineteenth century, as the British Empire expanded, it became common practice for the government to award medals to soldiers and sailors who participated in campaigns around the world.

As the century progressed the system was standardised as far as possible. Although major wars (such as the Crimean War of 1854–6 and the Afghan Wars) led to the issuing of distinct awards, the idea of a general service medal for 'small wars' was born. One medal would be awarded for campaign service in a particular area such as India, West Africa, Egypt or South Africa, with clasps added as and when the recipient qualified by further active service in the same region. This reduced the number of medals a soldier or sailor received for repeated campaigning in one area.

Although the principle of a general service medal continued into the twentieth century and is still current – for example, for service in Northern Ireland – the system would have been unwieldy during the two world wars, when there were too many major actions and potential recipients for the issuing of clasps to be extensively applied. On the grounds of expense, the awards for the First World War (1914–18) were *war* medals, for general service during the

Medal group reflecting service in the Boer War, 1899–1902, and First World War, 1914–18: Queen's and King's South Africa Medals with 1914 Star and clasp, the British War Medal and the Victory Medal. To the far right is the Army Long Service and Good Conduct Medal. The recipient of these awards, Gunner George Cave, was killed in action on the Somme in 1916.

whole war, rather than *campaign* medals for specific operations within the war. A similar system operated in the Second World War (1939–45), where *theatre of war* awards were made (for Africa, North-West Europe and the Pacific, for example) rather than medals for individual battles or campaigns, though a few clasps were awarded to the Second World War stars.

Today, with the decline of Britain's imperial commitments and the ending of the Cold War, British forces serve overseas as part of United Nations (UN) or North Atlantic Treaty Organisation (NATO) forces as well as on their own, thereby qualifying for the service medals introduced by those organisations in addition to specifically British awards.

The serious collecting of war medals began in the later nineteenth century, fuelled by an interest in Britain's imperial campaigns and those of the recent past, in particular the French Wars of 1793–1815. The first detailed reference books and collectors' magazines appeared in the period 1860–1900; most are now collectors' items in their own right, but many have been reprinted.

Thousands of collectors around the world are now involved in the hobby and, not surprisingly, they vary in their interests. Some collect single medals, others only groups – combinations of awards to one recipient reflecting extensive service. Some specialise in medals for a particular area such as South Africa, or for a single campaign such as Malaya, or even for a single battle such as El Alamein, and will try to build a collection representing medals and clasps for each unit engaged. Some collect medals to a particular regiment, corps, ship or squadron, building up a collection that charts its history. Others collect medals to recipients from their own area or, increasingly popular today, with the same surname as themselves.

The key to this is that the majority of British medals are officially named to their recipient and generally identify their regiment or unit. This enables the collector to search local or national archives and published reference books to piece together an individual career or the services of his or her military unit. The medal thus becomes a personalised link with the past: the collector can own something worn by someone who *was there* and participated in some of the memorable incidents in Britain's military history.

Basic terms

Campaign medals

Campaign medals are awards for service in a particular campaign or battle, given for being present within a designated area and time-span, without regard to the recipient's rank or achievements (in contrast to gallantry awards or decorations). Campaign medals are worn in chronological order of award, outwards from the centre of the wearer's left chest. Decorations and gallantry awards are worn to the left of the group (as viewed) and foreign awards to the right.

Medals are issued at formal parades and ceremonies or are sent by post, each medal within a small card box. They are also awarded to the designated next of kin of a recipient who was killed or died from any cause whilst on active service.

Clasps

These are single-faced metal bars attached directly to the medal (or in some later examples sewn on to the ribbon) indicating service in a particular campaign (for example *Iraq* or *Malaya*). Most carry side flanges to enable them to be fixed to the suspension and riveted to each other, so that new ones can be attached as earned. Usually the first-earned clasp is nearest the medal, so that the latest-earned is at the top, but clasps are occasionally found in the wrong order – perhaps sent to the recipient at a later date and attached wrongly – and often in a variety of unofficial ways, such as with wire.

As they were issued: boxes, packets and certificates issued with the Second World War stars and medals.

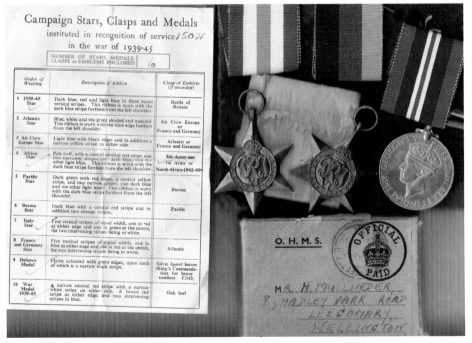

The principal parts and features of a medal.

Labels (on image): Ribbon, Clasp, Suspension, Swivel, Claw, Obverse, Reverse

Collectors commonly (though not strictly correctly) also refer to clasps as 'bars'.

New collectors should try to be sure that the clasps on a medal are the ones given to the recipient and not later additions by a soldier who wanted to claim more or added for fraudulent purposes. There was no limit to the number of clasps a man could wear on a particular medal – so long as he had earned them!

Materials

Most British awards are made of silver, though some later ones (especially those mass-produced for the two world wars or later UN or NATO medals) have been issued in cupro-nickel, bronze or various alloys. The majority of British campaign awards are circular, usually 36 mm in diameter.

Ribbons

Medals are worn suspended from their own specific ribbons, whose colours often have some heraldic or symbolic significance. Ribbons are usually 32 mm wide, and about 4 cm of ribbon are meant to show when worn, but many ribbons bearing a number of clasps would be longer and there seems never to have been a hard and fast usage amongst recipients.

Obverse

The side of the medal bearing the reigning monarch's effigy and titles or the Royal Cypher.

Reverse

The side of the medal bearing a decorative design, which may have a symbolic or allegorical meaning, or simply some form of wording. The designs were often put out to competition or tender and the designer's initials or name are sometimes found on the reverse.

Suspension

The means of fastening the ribbon and clasps to the medal disc by means of a bar attached to a claw or through a ring. Many British medals have swivelling suspensions – in other words the medal can be turned around to show either side whilst still displaying the correct side of the clasp. Medals are meant to be worn with the obverse (the monarch's effigy) facing the viewer. The suspension carrying the ribbon can be plain or ornamented. Stars have a simple ring suspension and were not designed to bear clasps, which are simply stitched on to the ribbon.

Naming

Most British medals are found named around the lower rim to their recipient – which is what makes the hobby so interesting to collectors. The details were added by machine in impressed capitals or (earlier on) by hand-engraving at the Royal Mint or the Calcutta Mint, both of which also made the medals and clasps. They usually include the recipient's number, rank and name, and regiment, branch of service or ship. Even where medals were issued unnamed (as, for example, with Second World War stars) they can be found privately named by their recipient. The beginner needs to learn to recognise the naming styles that are appropriate to the medal and *Suspensions: plain,* period, and to pick out the ones that have been altered or added later *ornamented and* to unnamed medals for fraudulent purposes. *ring.*

The Africa General Service Medal, 1902–56

Introduced in 1902 to standardise awards for minor campaigns in tropical Africa, it was still current in 1914 and nine later clasps were issued. The medal is never seen without a clasp and some are very rare, most being granted to local forces like the King's African Rifles. They continue the practice of bearing simply an area and date that was current before the First World War, as with *East Africa 1914*, *East Africa 1915* and *East Africa 1918*, all mainly for service against the Turkhana tribe. *Shimber Berris 1914–15* recalled service in two brief campaigns in November 1914 and February 1915 in which Indian troops were largely employed to destroy fortifications in Somaliland. *Nyasaland 1915* was granted mainly to the KAR and local volunteers for service during a rebellion in the Shire Highlands, whilst *Jubaland 1917–18* was awarded for operations against the Aulihan tribe along the Juba river. *Nigeria 1918* was granted for service during a revolt by the Egba tribe between Abeokuta and Lagos. *Somaliland 1920* was a much larger affair and commemorated the last of the campaigns against 'the Mad Mullah' (for which earlier *Somaliland* clasps had been issued) and was awarded to Army, Navy and Air Force personnel.

The last clasp awarded – fifty years after the medal was introduced and by far the most common – was *Kenya*, for service between 21st October 1952 and 17th November 1956 during the Emergency, declared as a result of the Mau-Mau rebellion by the Kikuyu tribe. A large number of British regiments and Royal Air Force squadrons received the medal.

There are no issues of the AGS bearing the effigy of King George VI.

Top right: Africa General Service Medal, 1902–56. Obverse with uncrowned head of Queen Elizabeth II. Clasp 'Kenya' for service in the Mau-Mau rebellion, 1952–6.

Bottom right: Africa General Service Medal, 1902–56. Reverse with a highly symbolic design depicting Britannia offering peace and law to Africa as a new day breaks.

9

The India General Service Medal, 1908–35

Inaugurated in 1908 for service in small campaigns in the Indian empire, two clasps had been issued before the First World War (*North West Frontier 1908* and *Abor 1911–12*). Most were awarded for fighting on the turbulent North West Frontier and the majority of its ten clasps issued after the First World War are easily available and relatively inexpensive. The first of these, *Afghanistan – NWF 1919*, was for the Third Afghan War of 1919 and related frontier operations. These involved some sizeable actions (including the first use of the RAF on the frontier), with the medal being awarded to large numbers of Indian and British units. After this, a series of clasps rewarded service in Waziristan – the area of most consistent opposition to British rule: *Waziristan 1919–21* and *Waziristan 1921–24* were awarded for operations against the Tochi and Wana Waziris, whilst the rarer *Mahsud 1919–20* was granted specifically for a difficult campaign against the Mahsud tribe, centred on Jandola; this clasp is generally seen with *Waziristan 1919–21*. Many British regiments, corps and ancillary units received these clasps, apart from *Mahsud 1919–20*, which was mainly awarded to Indian forces. By far the rarest

Right: The India General Service Medal, 1908–35. Standard reverse, showing the fortress of Jamrud, 'the Gateway to the Khyber Pass'. Most of its clasps rewarded service on the North West Frontier.

Wearing their medals: soldiers of the King's Shropshire Light Infantry in 1937. They all wear the 1908 India General Service Medal with clasp 'North West Frontier 1930–31' and the Coronation Medal for 1937. Three wear the 1914–18 British War Medal and Victory Medal and four have the Long Service and Good Conduct Medal.

clasp is *Waziristan 1925*, granted to a few RAF squadrons for bombing raids over hostile tribal territory. RAF personnel were, most unusually, given a choice of award: this one or *Waziristan 1921-24* if they had served within those dates. In the end only about 275 of these clasps were issued.

Two more unusual clasps – in that they were not for the North West Frontier – were *Malabar 1921-22* and *Burma 1930-32*. The former was for operations involving British and Indian units against the Moplahs of the Malabar coast of south-west India, who rose in rebellion in 1921. The latter was for service in a now forgotten but widespread Burmese rebellion along the Irrawaddy.

The last clasps on the 1908 IGS were for familiar frontier zones. *North West Frontier 1930-31* rewarded service in Waziristan, service against the Afridis on the Khajuri plain west of Peshawar, and service against 'Red Shirt' rebels north of Peshawar. *Mohmand 1933* was granted for operations against the Hill or Upper Mohmand tribe north-west of Peshawar (another consistent source of opposition to the British) whilst the last clasp issued, *North West Frontier 1935*, was for a difficult campaign against the Mohmands and around Loe Agra.

It is common to see medals to Indian recipients bearing multiple clasps, but most British soldiers received only one or two. The old practice of awarding bronze medals to Indian non-combatant 'followers' such as servants or grooms ceased after the clasp *Abor 1911-12*; all received the silver version after this date.

Above: The India General Service Medal, 1908–35. Obverse with George V, the type current between 1910 and 1930. Simple legend 'Kaisar-i-Hind' (Emperor of India). Multiple clasp awards like this are usually to Indian soldiers.

Left: The India General Service Medal, 1908–35. Obverse with the George V pattern current between 1930 and 1935 and standard abbreviated Latin titles. Clasps 'Burma 1930–32' and 'North West Frontier 1935'.

Awards for the
First World War,
1914–18

Some of the most appalling fighting ever experienced took place during the 'Great War'. The casualty figures and conditions of even the largest and most severe of earlier wars like the Crimean War, or colonial campaigns against the Zulu, the Boers or in India, pale into insignificance beside some of the battles on the Western Front and in theatres like Gallipoli or Mesopotamia. Numbers killed frequently reached into the tens of thousands and troops experienced levels of hardship which we can barely comprehend. Even the 'forgotten' fronts like East Africa, Italy or Salonika offer examples of severe fighting, often in atrocious conditions.

'Over the top':
British troops
advancing into
action at Ginchy on
the Somme in July
1916.

The 1914 Star

Authorised in April 1917, this simple bronze star bearing the date 'Aug–Nov 1914' rewarded the 'Old Contemptibles' – the original British Expeditionary Force (BEF) and their immediate reinforcements who crossed into Belgium and France in the earliest days of the war. Often, but incorrectly, known as the 'Mons Star', it was awarded to British soldiers and Royal Marines (but to very few sailors – only those who served on land) for the opening campaigns on the Western Front: most famous is the 'Retreat to Mons' in August 1914 and the fighting around Ypres. The reverse is plain and flat and bears the recipient's name and other details. Approximately 378,000 were awarded for service between 4th August 1914 (the day Britain declared war on Germany) and midnight of 22nd November. Although there was fighting elsewhere in 1914, notably in

Left: *The 1914 Star. Obverse, bearing the date 'Aug–Nov 1914'. Awarded for the first campaigns on the Western Front in Flanders and France but not for any other theatre of war.*

Below: *The 1914 Star. Reverse, showing typical Army naming details. Naval awards do not show the ship name, simply 'R.N.'.*

Mesopotamia, and at sea, this star was awarded only for land operations on the Western Front. Those serving in other theatres received the 1914–15 Star (see below). The 1914 Star was also awarded to imperial forces who served on the Western Front at this time.

All recipients of this medal automatically qualified as well for the British War Medal and Victory Medal (see below). In other words, they received three campaign awards.

The only clasp awarded with the 1914 Star was *5th Aug. – 22nd Nov. 1914.* It was granted to any soldier who had been 'under fire' between those dates. Its purpose was to distinguish those who had been in action from those who had worked behind the lines. Not sanctioned until 1919, most had to be claimed personally by the recipient, which explains why there are far fewer clasps than there were men who should have received one – many had been killed by 1918 or neglected to apply. When ribbons alone were worn, a silver rosette denoted entitlement to the clasp.

The clasp '5th Aug. – 22nd Nov. 1914' awarded with the 1914 Star to those who came under the close fire of the enemy. Unusually, the clasp is stitched directly on to the ribbon and is not attached to the medal.

The 1914–15 Star, obverse. Like the 1914 Star, the reverse is flat and plain and bears the recipient's number, rank, name and unit or branch of service.

The 1914–15 Star

This is one of the commonest campaign medals, easily available on the collectors' market. It was awarded for service around the world, in any theatre of war or at sea, to British forces of all kinds (military, naval and air, support, nursing and civilian) and to imperial troops from Canada, Australia, South Africa, India and New Zealand. However common, we should not forget that its wearers could have been involved in some of the most severe fighting of the war – in the Ypres Salient ('the worst place in the world' in 1915), on Gallipoli or in any of the other major campaigns such as Mesopotamia, Salonika, East Africa or in far-flung corners like West Africa, Persia and the North West Frontier. In many of these areas, disease and climate vied with the enemy to test the forces engaged. As with the 1914 Star, recipients were automatically entitled to the British War Medal and Victory Medal (see below), so ultimately received three campaign awards.

About 2,360,000 of these simple bronze stars were awarded and, like their 1914 counterpart, they are named on their plain reverse. The ribbon was identical to that of the 1914 Star. Since no-one could receive both stars, this was not expected to cause a problem, though some 1914 Star recipients were unhappy that there was no easily visible distinction between them and their later colleagues, unless they were wearing the 1914 clasp or the silver rosette denoting the clasp.

The British War Medal, 1914–18

The standard silver war medal for the First World War, the British War Medal was awarded to all forces of the Empire and given to anyone who had served in uniform or had rendered 'approved' service. Unlike the previous stars, it could be awarded singly – for example for service in garrison areas like Malta or India, or for certain categories of service in the United Kingdom. It was also awarded to foreign citizens who rendered service to the Allied cause. Although dated '1914–18', the medal was awarded to British forces involved in the Allied intervention in the Russian Civil War between 1918 and 1920.

Approximately 6,500,000 were issued to British and Imperial forces and to support services such as nurses, ambulance units and transport personnel, making the BWM the commonest British campaign award.

It was originally proposed that clasps would be issued, and lists were drawn up: sixty-eight for the Royal Navy and seventy-nine for the Army. Naval clasps would be granted for all sorts of actions around the world (for example *Falkland Islands 8 Dec 1914*, *Minesweeping* and *North Russia 1918–19*) whilst those to the army would commemorate some of the great land campaigns and epic battles of the war. From the collector's point of view, these clasps would have made an interesting addition, indicating a recipient's service, and many unusual combinations would no doubt have been possible. However, in 1923 the plan was scrapped on the grounds of cost, although one occasionally sees dress miniatures mounted with naval clasps.

Above left: The British War Medal, 1914–18, obverse. With over 6,500,000 issued, this is the commonest British campaign medal. The ribbon colours are supposed not to have any particular significance.

Above right: The British War Medal, 1914–18, reverse. Its symbolic design depicts a naked warrior, or possibly St George, on horseback, trampling the arms of the Central Powers and the emblems of Death. It is also said to symbolise Man's control over Nature and the forces of destruction.

The British War Medal, 1914–18, reverse of the bronze issue. Only 110,000 were awarded (to non-combatant units like the Chinese Labour Corps) and they are now quite scarce.

The BWM *in bronze* was awarded to members of various non-combatant labour corps – Chinese, Indian, Maltese – and the Macedonian Mule Corps. Many bronze BWMs have only the number and unit of the recipient around the rim, rather than his name.

The Victory Medal

This bronze, gilt-washed medal is also known as the Allied Victory Medal as the Allied nations agreed to issue a standardised medal and ribbon to their forces to avoid a mass exchange of medals between them. In other words, the Victory Medal of Great Britain is similar to that of France, Belgium, the USA, Japan and other Allies, and all bear a symbolic figure of Victory and the same rainbow-coloured ribbon. The reverse dates are '1914–1919', to include post-war intervention in the Russian Civil War. When awarded to South African forces, the medal carries a *bilingual reverse*, with the wording in both English and Afrikaans.

Approximately 5,725,000 were issued. They were never awarded by themselves and are often seen worn only with the British War Medal, awarded to those who served in a theatre of war after 1st January 1916 and who did not, therefore, qualify for one of the earlier bronze stars.

Far left: *The Victory Medal. Obverse, with winged Victory. Similar designs (and the same ribbon) were used for the victory medals of all the Allied countries.*

Left: *The Victory Medal, reverse. This medal is never seen worn by itself, but always in conjunction with at least the British War Medal or other 1914–18 awards.*

Far left: *Territorial Force War Medal, 1914–19, reverse. Although bearing the dates '1914–19', eligibility for the medal ceased on 11th November 1918, when the war ended.*

Left: *Territorial Force War Medal, 1914–19. Obverse, with 'coinage' head of George V. The ribbon combines the yellow of the old Imperial Yeomanry Long Service Medal and the green of the Volunteer Long Service Medal.*

The Territorial Force War Medal, 1914–19

This bronze medal was granted to members of the Territorial Force serving before August 1914 or who had four years' service, and who had undertaken prior to 30th September 1914 to serve overseas and had then served outside the United Kingdom. Entry into a theatre of war was not necessary: overseas garrison duty (for example in India) would count. It was not possible to receive this award and the 1914 or 1914–15 Star. As only 34,000 were issued it is the rarest of the general series for the First World War. Never awarded by itself, it is usually seen with the British War Medal (for those who did not serve in a theatre of war) or the BWM and Victory Medal (for those who saw active service), in which case it is worn after the Victory Medal.

The Mercantile Marine Medal, 1914–18

This bronze award, with its dramatic reverse scene, recognised the vital services of the Merchant Navy during the war. Just over 133,000 were awarded, with one or more voyages in a designated

Above: *The Mercantile Marine Medal, 1914–18, obverse. A bronze medal issued under the auspices of the Board of Trade. The colourful ribbon shows the port and starboard lights of a merchant vessel.*

The Mercantile Marine Medal, 1914–18. Reverse, depicting a merchant vessel ploughing through heavy seas, a sinking submarine in the foreground and a sailing ship in the distance.

'Just out of the trenches, Arras, March 1917': tired and caked in mud, soldiers of the King's Shropshire Light Infantry return from a tour in the front line.

war zone qualifying. Recipients who served only in the Merchant Navy received this medal and the British War Medal, but those who also served in other units during the war (such as those who joined the Royal Navy or Army) could also qualify for the 1915 Star and the Victory Medal, which meant they could wear up to four medals.

The Memorial Plaque

Although not a campaign medal, the bronze memorial plaque is such a familiar item that a reference is not out of place. Commonly called 'death plaques', they were given to the next of kin of anyone in the forces or associated services who was killed or died from any cause – wounds, accident or illness, at home or abroad – during the war and up to c.1921. They were also granted to the next of kin of casualties in Imperial forces; those of Canadian casualties also received a silver Memorial Cross (which was also awarded in the Second World War). Around 1,350,000 were issued, each with an illuminated commemorative scroll. A rare version, '*She* died ...', of which only about six hundred were issued, was given in respect of female casualties, mainly nurses.

The bronze Memorial Plaque, bearing the full name of the casualty but no details of rank, number or military unit.

General Service awards

The Naval General Service Medal, 1915–62

Instituted in 1915, this attractive medal was intended for Royal Navy and Royal Marine personnel involved in purely naval operations. Its first clasp was retrospective: *Persian Gulf 1909–14* was granted for operations against gunrunners shipping arms from Arabia to the already turbulent North West Frontier via Baluchistan. Although Indian army units served ashore, the clasp was awarded only to Royal Navy and Royal Marine personnel and to a handful of Indian Army officers serving aboard warships.

Many of the later clasps mirror those of the 1918 General Service Medal (see below), reflecting offshore naval support of land operations. Examples are *S.E. Asia 1945–46*, *Palestine 1936–39*, *Palestine 1945–48*, *Malaya* (on medals with the George VI or Elizabeth II obverse for service offshore between 1948 and 1960), *Near East* (for the Suez Crisis, 1956), *Cyprus* (for service 1955–9), and *Arabian Peninsula* (for service 1957–60). *Brunei* was granted for operations in December 1962, many going to Royal Marines of 42 Commando.

Some clasps are more specifically naval. The very rare *Iraq 1919–20* was given only to the crews of a few small river gunboats for service between 1st July and 17th November 1920 (so it is difficult to see why '1919' features in the date). Only 128 were awarded. *N.W. Persia 1919–20* is exceptionally rare, awarded to members of a naval mission to north-west Persia and to Baku on the Caspian Sea.

Above left: The Naval General Service Medal, 1915–62. Obverse of Queen Elizabeth II. Clasp 'Near East' for the Suez Crisis of 1956.

Above right: The Naval General Service Medal, 1915–62, reverse. This attractive design shows Britannia drawn by seahorses on a chariot of shells.

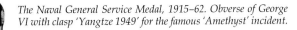

Recipients were asked to exchange the award for the correctly dated, and equally rare, clasp *N.W. Persia 1920*. A particularly famous and interesting event is recalled by *Yangtze 1949*, when HMS *Amethyst* was trapped in the Yangtze in April 1949 by Chinese Communist forces. In a famous escape, she fought her way down river and rejoined the fleet. The crews of other ships that attempted to come to her aid (*London, Black Swan* and *Consort*) also received the award, as did a very few RAF and Army personnel. The ships are not named on the medal, but those attributable to the *Amethyst* are especially sought after.

Three clasps reflect truly difficult work in the aftermath of a world war: *Minesweeping 1945–51* and *Bomb and Mine Clearance 1945–53* were granted for work in bomb and mine disposal in various parts of the world, whilst the very rare *B & M Clearance, Mediterranean* was given primarily for bomb and mine disposal work in and around Malta. As six months' consecutive service was required to qualify – a long time in these dangerous activities – they are all scarce, with issues of only 4,750 of the first, 145 of the second and about 60 of the last.

The NGS medal ceased to be issued after 1962 when naval personnel became eligible for the new General Service Medal of 1962, which standardised awards amongst the three services (see below).

The General Service Medal, 1918–62

Instituted in 1923, this was the land equivalent of the Naval General Service Medal and rewarded operations in small wars around the British Empire after 1918. Sixteen clasps were issued, many of which are common, and multiple combinations are seen. The first clasps were issued for what was very much the aftermath of the First World War. *Iraq* was granted for the difficult operations between 10th December 1919 and 17th November 1920 during the Arab revolt against the post-war British occupation of Mesopotamia. It was awarded to a large number of British and Indian units, those to the Manchester Regiment for the disastrous action at Hillah on 24th July 1920 being especially sought after. *Kurdistan* was awarded for

General Service Medal, 1918–62. Reverse, showing the backstrap of a clasp. The symbolic design shows Britannia (as a winged Victory) placing a laurel wreath on emblems of the RAF and Army.

General Service Medal, 1918–62, George V obverse. With clasp 'S. Persia', awarded for tribal operations in 1918–19, usually to Indian soldiers – very few British personnel received this clasp.

operations between 23rd May and 6th December 1919 against nationalist Kurds in northern Iraq, who demanded their own homeland after the defeat of Turkey in 1918. It was also issued for further operations between 19th March and 18th June 1923 – the first time that troops were airlifted into action. *S. Persia* was granted for operations between 12th November 1918 and 22nd June 1919 and *N.W. Persia* for operations between 10th August and 31st December 1920, including operations along the Caspian coast against Bolshevik forces. Indian Army units were largely the recipients of these two clasps.

Two rare awards, *Southern Desert Iraq* for operations between 8th January and 3rd June 1928 and *Northern Kurdistan*, between 15th March and 21st June 1932, were granted almost exclusively to the RAF units which, with local levies, largely took over the role of the Army in dealing with tribal operations in remote, inhospitable areas.

Palestine was given for service during the Arab revolt against Jewish immigration into the British Mandated Territory between 1936 and 1939, and *Palestine 1945–48* for the continuation of those hostilities and clashes with Jewish settlers and immigrants prior to the British withdrawal and the creation of the state of Israel in 1948.

The clasp *S.E. Asia 1945–46* was granted mainly to Indian forces for regaining the Dutch East Indies and French Indo-China following the Japanese occupation and the growth of anti-European nationalist and communist groups. This was the last award to the British Indian Army: the sub-continent was granted independence in 1947. The common clasp *Malaya*, for anti-communist operations in the jungles of Malaya, covered the long period 1948–60 and is seen on the medal with obverses of George VI and Elizabeth II. *Cyprus* was given for anti-terrorist service on the island during the violent struggle for union with Greece led by Archbishop Makarios waged between 1st April 1955 and 18th April 1959. *Near East* was granted for one day's service during the militarily effective but politically disastrous Suez Crisis between October and December 1956. Following President Nasser's nationalisation of the Suez Canal, an Anglo-French force seized the canal zone but was subsequently halted by international pressure. *Arabian Peninsula*, for operations between 1st January 1957 and 30th June 1960, was awarded to British and local forces fighting in

Centre right:: *General Service Medal, 1918–62, George VI obverse. With clasp 'S.E. Asia 1945–46'. This clasp was largely awarded to Indian soldiers.*

Right: *General Service Medal, 1918–62, obverse, with clasp 'Malaya'. Because of the protracted nature of the jungle campaign (1948–60) this clasp can be found on medals with obverse of George VI or Elizabeth II.*

aid of the Sultan of Muscat during a rebellion by the Emir of Oman. *Brunei* was given for services in aid of the Sultan of Brunei in overcoming Indonesian aggression in December 1962 and was awarded to British (mainly Gurkha), Australian, New Zealand and local forces who served for one day or more in Brunei, North Borneo or Sarawak.

Two scarce clasps echo those on the Naval General Service Medal: *Bomb and Mine Clearance 1945–49* and *Bomb and Mine Clearance 1945–56* were granted for the dangerous task of clearing minefields and arms dumps created during the Second World War.

The 1918 GSM was superseded in 1962 by the new General Service Medal (see page 32).

However, an unusual retrospective award was approved in October 2003 in the form of the clasp *Canal Zone*. This was eventually authorised after a long national campaign by veterans and forces groups, initially in the teeth of official opposition. It is to be granted to those who served within the Suez Canal zone between October 1951 and October 1954. Remarkably, it is estimated that there may be up to 200,000 potential recipients. If the recipient already has the GSM with clasp, the new one will be fitted below or above the existing clasp, in correct chronological sequence. If the recipient does not already possess the GSM, the award will be made on the medal with the reverse of Queen Elizabeth II current in the 1950s. The award is not granted posthumously, even for those who were killed in action during the often arduous service in the zone at a time of growing Arab nationalism and anti-British feeling, which culminated in the Suez Crisis of 1956.

Above: *The 1918 General Service Medal with the retrospective clasp 'Canal Zone'. The obverse (shown) carries the titles of the Queen as used on the last issue of the medal in the 1950s, omitting 'Britt. Omn'.*

The India General Service Medal, 1936–9

This was the last in the long line of India General Service Medals issued before Indian independence in 1947. Its two clasps, *North West Frontier 1936–37* and *North West Frontier 1937–39* (commonly seen on one medal), were awarded for some arduous fighting in Waziristan and against the followers of the Islamic leader, the Fakir of Ipi. Many British regiments and RAF squadrons, and large numbers of Indian units of all kinds, received this medal. The IGSM represents a great deal of hard campaigning and would provide the basis for an interesting and inexpensive collection. Those produced by the Royal Mint in London are more finely detailed than those of the Calcutta Mint.

Far left: *The India General Service Medal, 1936–9, obverse, showing the two clasps issued with this medal, both for service on the North West Frontier.*

Left: *The India General Service Medal, 1936–9, reverse. This one shows the slightly less detailed Calcutta Mint version, as issued to Indian troops.*

Awards for the Second World War, 1939–45

Campaign service during the Second World War was rewarded by a series of eight stars, reminiscent of those for 1914 and 1914–15. No more than five could be worn by any one recipient, further service being represented by clasps sewn on to the ribbon, and no recipient could wear more than one clasp on any one star. When ribbons alone are worn, clasps are usually denoted by a silver rosette on the appropriate ribbon.

An example of the clasps issued with the 1939–45 stars, in this case '8th Army', awarded with the Africa Star. These plain clasps are stitched directly on to the ribbon. Only one clasp may be worn on any star.

The copper-zinc alloy stars were plain on the reverse but unusually, on the grounds of expense, were issued unnamed to British forces. Stars to South African, Indian (but not Pakistani) and Australian recipients were named or otherwise personalised by their own governments. Recalling as they do some of the great battles and campaigns of the Second World War – Dunkirk, Singapore, El Alamein, Monte Cassino, Kohima, D-Day and many others – it is regretted by collectors that the stars bear no personal details and thus lose something of their historical connection unless they

A group of 4th King's Shropshire Light Infantry in London for the Jubilee of the Territorial Army in 1958. Most wear campaign stars and medals for 1939–45. A few wear the 1918 GSM and one (rear, far right) has Korean War medals.

The 1939–45 Star. Ribbon stripes in colours of the three services: dark blue (Royal Navy), red (Army), sky blue (RAF).

happen to form part of a group containing a named award or gallantry medal.

The ribbons were reputedly designed by King George VI and generally have a heraldic or symbolic significance.

The 1939–45 Star

This was the basic overseas war-service star for the Second World War and was originally to be dated 1939–43. Servicemen generally had to complete six months' active service (two months for operational aircrews) to qualify for this star before they could count time towards a theatre of war award. The 1939–45 Star was the sole campaign star awarded to men who saw service only in France in 1939–40 (including the Dunkirk operations), Norway in 1940, Greece or Crete, or in various commando raids (St Nazaire, Dieppe) and who did not serve overseas other than that.

One clasp, *Battle of Britain*, was awarded to 'the Few', the RAF personnel of the sixty-one fighter squadrons engaged in the Battle of Britain between 10th July and 31st October 1940. When ribbons alone are worn, this clasp is denoted by a gilt (not silver) rosette. Collectors should be aware that this rare clasp has been extensively faked.

The Atlantic Star (3rd September 1939 to 8th May 1945)

This star rewarded those who served in the Battle of the Atlantic, maintaining supplies to the United Kingdom and her Allies by convoy against the assaults of the German navy and U-boat fleet. It was granted mainly to Royal and Merchant Navy personnel but was also earned by some RAF squadrons and by Army personnel such as Royal Artillery gunners on armed merchantmen. Recipients had to have qualified for the 1939–45 Star before their theatre service (usually six months) counted towards this award. Those who subsequently qualified for the Air Crew Europe or the France and Germany Stars would wear the appropriate clasp. However, only one clasp (the first earned) could be worn.

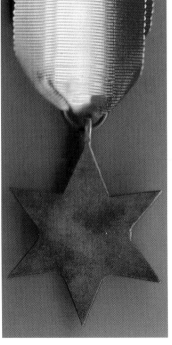

The standard plain reverse of all the Second World War stars (in this case the Atlantic Star). They are sometimes found privately engraved with personal details.

Left: *The Air Crew Europe Star. The light blue of the ribbon represents the sky with black stripes representing the night and yellow for searchlight beams.*

Below: *The Africa Star. The ribbon bears the colours of the three services (with red for the Army being the widest, in token of the major part they played) on a background representing the desert.*

The Air Crew Europe Star (3rd September 1939 to 5th June 1944)

This star was awarded to RAF air-crews for operational flights from Britain over Europe. The 1939–45 Star had to have been earned before the two-months' qualifying time for this award counted. Those who later qualified for the Atlantic or France and Germany Stars wore a clasp denoting the first earned; they did not receive the additional stars and could only wear one clasp. This star is the scarcest in the series and has been widely faked.

The Africa Star (10th June 1940 to 12th May 1943)

This was conferred for one or more days' service in North Africa during the above period. It rewarded service against the Italians in Abyssinia, Somaliland, Eritrea and the Sudan, or against German and Italian forces (principally Rommel's *Afrika Korps*) in Egypt, Libya, Tunisia and Morocco. Naval service and escort duty off the coasts also counted, as did service on the island of Malta, which famously received the George Cross for its gallant defence against relentless enemy air attacks. Service in West Africa and Madagascar did not qualify for this award.

Three clasps were granted, only one of which could be worn. *North Africa 1942–43* was awarded mainly to the Royal and Merchant Navy personnel who served inshore or on escort duty between 23rd October 1942 and 12th May 1943 and to RAF crews for service in or over North Africa during that time. *1st Army* was granted to men of that force for service in Tunisia or Algeria between 8th November and 31st December 1942, and elsewhere to 12th May 1943, whilst *8th Army* went to soldiers of that army for service between 23rd October 1942 (the date of the decisive battle of El Alamein) and 12th May 1943, the effective end of the campaign in North Africa. When ribbons alone are worn, the *1st Army* clasp is represented by a silver numeral '1', and the *8th Army* by a numeral '8'. A silver rose emblem was worn by staff of the headquarters of 18th Army Group who did not qualify for either army clasp and to various South African units. The 1939–45 Star did not have to be earned as a prerequisite for the award of this star.

The Pacific Star (8th December 1941 to 2nd September 1945)

This rather scarce award was granted for service in a number of areas, including Malaya in 1941 and Singapore before its fall in January 1942, in Hong Kong prior to its capture in December 1941 and in the Pacific during the later reconquest of Japanese-occupied islands and territories. Army and RAF personnel were not required to have earned the 1939–45 Star, but Royal and Merchant Navy recipients were, unless their entry into the theatre was too late to fulfil the time qualification. Many of these stars went to Commonwealth forces (of whom some became prisoners of war) or to naval forces engaged in the Pacific islands campaigns. Those who subsequently earned the Burma Star wore the clasp *Burma* on the ribbon of the Pacific Star; they did not receive both medals.

The Burma Star (11th December 1941 to 2nd September 1945)

The Burma Star was granted for service during the often ferocious fighting against the Japanese in Burma from the time of their initial onslaught, which drove Imperial forces back to the Indian frontier in 1941, until the campaign of reconquest prior to the surrender of Japan in September 1945. The difficult jungle, river and hill terrain, the weather and tropical diseases all had to be endured. The award also encompassed fighting in Assam and Bengal during the initial Japanese attack, and later service on the Chinese frontier. Service in Malaya during its reconquest also qualified, but not that in 1941 prior to the fall of Singapore, for which the Pacific Star was awarded. In addition to British Army, Navy and Air Force recipients, many units of the Indian Army and other Commonwealth forces received this star. Royal and Merchant Navy

The Pacific Star. Ribbon colours of the three services, with yellow for the island beaches and green for the jungle.

The Burma Star. Awarded for the exceptionally difficult campaign in Burma and surrounding areas to reconquer British territories taken by the Japanese.

Below: *The Italy Star. No clasps were awarded with this star. The ribbon shows the heraldic colours of Italy.*

recipients had to have earned the 1939–45 Star first, unless their service came too late in the war to allow for the necessary time qualification. Those who subsequently qualified for the Pacific Star wore the clasp *Pacific*; they did not receive both stars.

The Italy Star (11th June 1943 to 8th May 1945)

This was intended to reward service in Italy from the invasion of Pantellaria and Sicily until the end of the war but, despite its title, it was also granted for operational service in the Aegean, the Dodecanese, Corsica, Elba, Greece, Sardinia, Yugoslavia, southern France and Austria. Royal and Merchant Navy personnel had to have qualified for the 1939–45 Star before they could earn this award, unless they served late in the war and could not build up the time necessary for the 1939–45 Star; Army and RAF personnel did not need to have earned the 1939–45 Star prior to qualifying. No clasps were issued with this award.

The France and Germany Star. The ribbon is in the colours of the Allies: Britain, France and the USA.

The France and Germany Star (4th June 1944 to 8th May 1945)

Despite its name, this was the theatre award for all North-West Europe, including Belgium and Holland, during the campaigns of 1944–5. Service in southern France in 1944–5 was rewarded with the Italy Star. Recipients of this medal did not need to qualify for the 1939–45 Star as a prerequisite. Awarded for some of the most dangerous and decisive operations of the war – notably the D-Day landings – and for the liberation of occupied countries in western Europe, this star could be granted to Army, Royal and Merchant Navy, and RAF personnel. Recipients who subsequently qualified for the Atlantic Star wore the clasp *Atlantic* on the ribbon; they could not receive both stars. There was no clasp *Air Crew Europe* for this star.

The Defence Medal

This unnamed cupro-nickel medal was awarded for the defence of Britain during a time of threatened enemy

Above left: *The Defence Medal, reverse. The ribbon is said to symbolise England's 'green and pleasant land' under blackout (black stripes) and air attack (flame-coloured stripe).*

Above right: *The Defence Medal, obverse, with the uncrowned head of George VI.*

Above left: *The 1939–45 War Medal, reverse. A lion standing in triumph over a double-headed dragon.*
Above right: *The 1939–45 War Medal, obverse. Crowned head of George VI. The ribbon is in the familiar red, white and blue colours of Great Britain.*

invasion and heavy air attacks. It was granted to members of military, civilian, medical and other forces (notably the Home Guard) who rendered three years' service at home. It could also be granted to those who served overseas in areas threatened by or subject to enemy air attacks. Service in Ceylon, Malta, Gibraltar, Cyprus, West Africa and parts of the Middle East qualified. It could be awarded by itself or in combination with other Second World War awards. Those issued by the Canadian government are solid silver.

The 1939–45 War Medal

The standard war medal for the Second World War, this common cupro-nickel medal was granted to anyone who rendered twenty-eight days' service in uniform or in an accredited organisation. It could be awarded by itself to those who did not qualify for any other campaign award or the Defence Medal. As with the Defence Medal, those issued by the Canadian government are in solid silver. Some Commonwealth countries – India, South Africa, Canada, Australia, New Zealand, Southern Rhodesia and (as late as 1981) Newfoundland – awarded their own distinctive 1939–45 War Medal to their forces in addition to this medal.

A display of medals and memorabilia relating to the Korean War in the Shropshire Regimental Museum, Shrewsbury Castle.

Medals for the Korean War,
1951–3

The first 'UN war', this was also the first conflict faced by the Great Powers since the end of the Second World War and in the nuclear age. A North Korean invasion of South Korea in June 1950 was countered by the dispatch of UN (largely American) forces, who drove back the invaders and pressed on into North Korea towards China. This led to China's entry into the conflict and the whole campaign escalated far beyond its original dimensions. The most famous British action is the defence of the Imjin river positions by the Gloucester Regiment on 25th May 1951; medals to those known to have been present are highly sought after, as are those to winners of gallantry awards.

The cupro-nickel **Korean War Medal** was awarded for one day's service in Korea or twenty-eight days' service offshore. No clasps were issued. It is sometimes referred to as the Queen's Korea Medal to distinguish it from the medal issued to all UN soldiers who fought in Korea.

Far left: *Korean War Medal, obverse, with the uncrowned head of Elizabeth II. This was the first campaign medal to bear the new Queen's effigy, George VI having died in 1952 whilst the war was still in progress. There are two obverse types: with 'Britt. Omn.' in the Queen's titles or without, whilst those to Canadian forces also have 'Canada' on the obverse.*

Left: *Korean War Medal, reverse design, which shows Hercules fighting the Hydra, symbolising the struggle against the spread of communism.*

UN soldiers also received the bronze **UN Korea Medal**, issued unnamed, with integral clasp *Korea*. Those to British forces are worn immediately after the Queen's medal; since Britain served as part of the UN force, it does not count as a foreign award. When personnel served in Korea only after the conclusion of the armistice (and up to 27th July 1954) they did not qualify for the British award and the UN Korea Medal is therefore sometimes seen without the Queen's medal.

Right: *The UN Korea Medal, obverse. It bears the badge of the UN and integral clasp 'Korea'. The ribbon colours are those of the UN.*

The UN Korea Medal, reverse. The reverse was struck in twelve different languages, reflecting the major languages of the UN.

31

The General Service Medal, 1962

Introduced in 1962 to replace both the 1915 Naval General Service Medal and the 1918 General Service Medal (see above), this medal was also intended to reward service in small wars and what were really the last of Britain's colonial campaigns. It is also known as the **Campaign Service Medal**. It has been awarded with thirteen clasps to date, most of which are common. Usually service of thirty days in the operational zone qualified.

The first clasp was *Borneo*, for service against Indonesian forces attempting to overrun Borneo between December 1962 and August 1966. Two clasps were awarded for service in and around Aden. *South Arabia* (August 1964 to November 1967) was largely for anti-terrorist operations around Britain's important naval base at the mouth of the Red Sea and in the Federation of South Arabia before independence. The scarcer *Radfan* (April to July 1964) was awarded for fourteen days' service during the effective British action against insurgents operating under Yemeni and Egyptian influence on the borders of the Federation of South Arabia, especially in the Radfan district; it is usually seen with *South Arabia*. *Malay Peninsula* (August 1964 to August 1966) was awarded for what was really a continuation of the Borneo operations, since Indonesian forces had also penetrated Malaya and a jungle campaign was undertaken along the peninsula. The very rare clasp *South Vietnam* (December 1962 to May 1964) was awarded to only sixty-eight members of the Australian Army Training Team, working with the forces of the Republic of South Vietnam (Australian and New Zealand forces actively engaged in the later Vietnam War received their own campaign medals).

The longest-running clasp to any British campaign medal is *Northern Ireland*; over 130,000 have been issued to date. It is awarded for service of at least thirty

Top: General Service Medal, 1962, obverse, with clasp 'Northern Ireland'. Covering peacekeeping duties between 1969 and the present day, this is the longest-running clasp ever issued. The Queen wears the low 'Tudor crown'.

Left: General Service Medal, 1962, reverse, showing clasps 'Radfan' and 'South Arabia' for operations around Aden, 1964–7. The medal is often referred to as the Campaign Service Medal (CSM) because of its reverse wording, shown here.

General Service Medal, 1962, obverse, with the clasp 'Gulf', largely awarded to naval forces for patrols in the Persian Gulf during the Iran–Iraq War.

days with British peacekeeping forces in Ulster since August 1969.

Despite its lengthy time-span (October 1969 to September 1976) the clasp *Dhofar* is somewhat scarce. It was given for service in aid of the Sultan of Oman in the Dhofar area against rebels backed by communist South Yemen. Many were awarded to the Special Air Service (SAS) and RAF personnel.

The rare clasp *Lebanon* (February 1983 to March 1984) was given to approximately 700 personnel who served in the multinational peacekeeping force sent into Beirut in the wake of the Israeli invasion of Lebanon to suppress Palestine Liberation Organisation bases. Since a lasting peace remained unlikely in the turmoil which followed, the force was withdrawn by March 1984. *Mine Clearance – Gulf of Suez* (15th August to 15th October 1984) was granted to naval forces engaged in minesweeping operations.

More recent clasps relate to events in the Persian Gulf region. *Gulf* (November 1986 to February 1989) was awarded largely to naval personnel manning British ships patrolling the Persian Gulf during the Iran–Iraq War. The rare clasp *Kuwait* was for service between March and September 1991 in the aftermath of the Gulf War. *N. Iraq & S. Turkey* is for forces (mainly RAF) involved in securing the 'no-fly' security zone over the Kurdish territories of Iraq following the Gulf War, and *Air Operations Iraq* is for RAF personnel involved in other patrols over Iraq. These latest four clasps are likely to become rarities on the collectors' market since relatively few have been awarded.

This medal was replaced in 1999 by the new **Operational Service Medal** (see page 38), though it should be noted that the 1962 GSM with clasps *Air Operations Iraq* and *Northern Ireland* will continue to be issued for the time being.

The 1962 General Service Medal (reverse) with the latest clasp, 'Air Operations Iraq', awarded to air forces patrolling Iraqi airspace after 16th July 1991.

The Rhodesia Medal,
1979–80

Though not strictly speaking a 'campaign medal', this award was granted to British troops (and to civilians and police) who took part in the supervision of the Rhodesian elections in 1980. Under the leadership of Ian Smith, the British colony made a 'Unilateral Declaration of Independence' (UDI) in 1965 and a long and often bloody civil war followed as African nationalist parties struggled to seize power. Eventually Smith's government collapsed and it was agreed that elections should be held to set up a new government and establish an independent state, to be called Zimbabwe. As so many armed factions were involved in the struggle for power, it was felt that a neutral force should supervise the whole process. This medal was granted for at least fourteen days service between 1st December 1979 and 20th March 1980 monitoring the elections. Since comparatively few British service personnel were involved, this is a rare award.

The medal bears the new 'Jubilee head' and titles of the Queen (see page 35) on its obverse. The reverse depicts a sable antelope, with the words 'The Rhodesia Medal 1980'. Only those awarded to Army and RAF personnel are officially named; the others are not. It should be noted that the cupro-nickel medal was rhodium plated, which gives it a particularly hard and brilliant surface.

The 1980 Rhodesia Medal, reverse, showing the sable antelope.

The South Atlantic Medal, 1982

This medal was awarded for the campaign of April to July 1982 to recover the Falkland Islands following the Argentinian invasion. Some thirty thousand were issued. The medal is cupro-nickel and bears the new 'Jubilee head' of the Queen. There were no clasps, but those who served on the Falklands or south of Ascension Island received a silver rosette, borne on the medal ribbon. Awards to the Parachute Regiment and Welsh Guards are highly sought after. Many medals were awarded to warships and to merchant and auxiliary ships; unusually for modern medals, the ship is named on the rim. Those to the submarine *Conqueror*, which sank the Argentine cruiser *General Belgrano*, and other warships heavily engaged are highly collectable.

Left: *The South Atlantic Medal for the Falklands campaign, 1982. Reverse, with coat of arms of the islands. The rosette worn on the ribbon denotes service actually in the Falklands or south of Ascension Island.*

Below: *The South Atlantic Medal, obverse. The Queen wears the high St Edward's Crown, first introduced on the Jubilee Medal of 1977 and hence known as the 'Jubilee head'.*

The Gulf Medal,
1990–1

The area of operation qualifying for this medal is very large, incorporating many areas of the Middle East and Cyprus. It was essentially granted for thirty days' service, including the campaign against Iraqi forces following their invasion of Kuwait in August 1990. The cupro-nickel medal, of which over 45,000 were awarded, bears on its reverse a combined services' emblem with dates '1990–91', whilst the obverse bears the 'Jubilee head' of the Queen.

The clasp *16 Jan to 28 Feb 1991* was granted for seven days' service in the forces which crossed the Iraqi frontier from Kuwait, whilst the rare clasp *2 August 1990* was issued to the small number of British servicemen in the Kuwait Liaison Team who were in Kuwait when the Iraqi invasion began.

Recipients of the Gulf Medal also received a medal from Saudi Arabia and from Kuwait, but these allied awards are not allowed to be worn in uniform (unlike awards of the nineteenth century such as the Turkish Crimean Medal and Khedive's Stars).

Above: *Buglers of the Royal Regiment of Fusiliers: the soldier in the foreground wears the Gulf Medal and the 1962 General Service Medal, clasp 'Northern Ireland'.*

Above: *The rare clasp '2 August 1990' awarded to the few British service personnel who were serving in Kuwait at the time of the Iraqi invasion of 1990.*

Far left: *The Gulf Medal, obverse, with the 'Jubilee head' of the Queen, and the clasp '16 Jan to 28 Feb 1991' and a ribbon with the rosette worn to indicate the award of the clasp.*

Left: *The Gulf Medal, reverse, with emblems of the three services. The ribbon has the colours of the three services on a desert background. This also shows the clasp reverse and pin-brooch from which the medal is worn.*

The Accumulated Campaign Service Medal,
1994 to date

This rather unusual medal, effectively for 'long service on campaign', was instituted in January 1994. It was granted to those holders of the 1962 General Service Medal who have completed an *accumulated* 'operational service' of thirty-six months since 14th August 1969. Its original purpose was to reward those who had done multiple tours of duty in Northern Ireland but who would have only one medal, the 1962 GSM with single clasp *Northern Ireland*, to show for all their service. Clasps may be awarded for further periods of thirty-six months. Service with NATO and United Nations forces does not count towards the award.

The obverse carries the standard 'Jubilee head' and titles of the monarch, while the reverse has a spray of oak and laurel branches with the words 'For Accumulated Campaign Service'.

The silver medal was the first medal to be manufactured by private contractors (rather than by the Royal Mint) and as such carries hallmarks on the rim, as well as the usual naming details.

The Accumulated Campaign Service Medal, reverse. The ribbon is simply that of the existing 1962 General Service Medal with a central gold stripe added.

37

The Operational Service Medal,
1999 to date

By 1999, the 1962 General Service Medal (see page 32) had been in existence for over thirty years and had been awarded with thirteen separate clasps. It was felt that the time had come to replace it with a new general service medal, the result being the **Operational Service Medal**, awarded for active operations after 5th May 2000.

The new silver medal bears on its obverse the usual 'Jubilee head' and titles of the monarch. The reverse features the Union Flag surrounded by a band with the words 'For operational service', superimposed on an eight-pointed star with different crowns (representing the different branches of the Armed Forces) on four arms. The medal is named with the recipient's details around the rim.

The standard obverse and reverse of the 1999 Operational Service Medal.

The original intention was to do away with clasps and, like the current United Nations and NATO medals, to indicate the area of operations simply by means of a distinct ribbon. In other words, a recipient might end up with three or four *identical* medals, each with a distinctive ribbon which alone denoted the various areas of service.

The first issue was for operations in Sierra Leone. British forces entered the country in May 2000 in the wake of a long and destructive civil war, their aim being to protect or evacuate British or European Union personnel if necessary. Intervention was meant to be brief but in January 2001, with the effective end of the fighting, it was announced that a small British presence (about four hundred) would be

The Operational Service Medal, reverse, with ribbon for service in Sierra Leone.

Soldiers of The Light Infantry on patrol near Freetown during Operation Silkman, one of a number of British operations following intervention in the civil war in Sierra Leone in 2001.

maintained, its role being primarily to train a new Sierra Leone army which would ensure peace and stability in the country.

The new medal was awarded for thirty days continuous service within Sierra Leone (or forty-five days in related operations outside the country) during Operations Basilica or Silkman or fourteen days continuous service within Sierra Leone (or twenty-one days in related operations outside the country) during Operation Palliser. Air forces could earn the medal for one day's service or one sortie during Operations Maidenly or Barras.

The Operational Service Medal has also been issued, with a distinctive ribbon, to British forces serving in Afghanistan after 11th September 2001. After the devastating civil war which led to Taliban control of that country and the impact of the 11th September attacks in the United States, it was decided to send international forces to Afghanistan to restore order and to destroy the Taliban movement. British forces (initially approximately 1500 strong) entered the country on 15th November 2001, supported by a powerful fleet in the Persian Gulf and air forces operating from other bases in the region. They served as part of the eighteen-nation International Security Assistance Force or ISAF (see also NATO awards, page 43) and ultimately helped to restore order and establish an interim government. British forces remain in Afghanistan

A British paratrooper mans a machine-gun post near Kabul following the intervention in Afghanistan by an international force in November 2001. This was the first time that British soldiers had fought around Kabul since 1880.

Part of the large British naval and air task force based in the Persian Gulf in support of operations in Afghanistan. They receive the Afghanistan Operational Service Medal without clasp.

as part of the multi-national presence supporting the new Afghan administration.

Interestingly, the initial intention of not awarding clasps to the Operational Service Medal has already been overridden. Since the medal was to be awarded to all those who had *supported* operations in Afghanistan (for example, air and naval forces operating from neighbouring areas), it was felt that land forces 'on the ground' in Kabul and elsewhere within the country should receive a more distinct award, reflecting the fact that they had served under circumstances of greater danger. It was therefore decided in October 2003 to issue the clasp *Afghanistan* to those who had actually served within the country and award the medal without clasp to those who had not.

Far left: The Operational Service Medal (reverse) with ribbon for Afghanistan. This is the medal without clasp, as awarded to support services stationed outside the country.

Left: The Operational Service Medal (obverse) with ribbon for Afghanistan. This bears the clasp 'Afghanistan' as awarded to British personnel serving 'on the ground' in that country.

The Iraq Medal, 2003

The Iraq Medal was awarded to British forces who served in Kuwait and Iraq during 'Operation Telic' from 20th January 2003. This operation was initially intended to overthrow the government of Saddam Hussein and establish a democratic regime in Iraq. Those who crossed the Iraqi frontier and served in the actual invasion and subsequent fighting were awarded the clasp *19th Mar to 28th Apr 2003*.

The multi-national occupation, spearheaded by US forces centred on Baghdad and with British troops based in the southern area around Basra, continues under increasingly difficult circumstances of civil unrest and active opposition from armed insurgent groups. British forces who continue to serve in the occupation and in operations against insurgents receive the medal without clasp.

The obverse of the cupro-nickel medal bears the usual effigy and titles of the monarch. The reverse, designed by Major M. Atkinson, depicts the human-headed winged bull or *Lamassu* of ancient Assyrian mythology, over the word 'Iraq'. The symbolism is reminiscent of that on the 1882 Egypt Medal, with its sphinx and date. The medal has the recipient's name and other details around the rim.

The Iraq Medal (reverse) with dated bar as awarded to those who served in the initial invasion of Iraq in 2003. It was awarded without clasp for later service.

British soldiers on patrol near Basra in the British zone of occupation in 2004.

41

UN and NATO awards

The United Nations Service Medal, 1957 to date

With forces from the United Kingdom playing an increasing role in UN peacekeeping and humanitarian missions across the globe, more and more British service personnel are earning the current UN awards. Generally ninety days' service is required to qualify. After the UN medal for Korea (see above), the next UN medal earned by British forces was for peacekeeping service on Cyprus, where conflict had arisen between the Greek and Turkish populations. This medal, first issued in 1964, is still current. To date over fifty UN medals have been issued, with British forces earning in particular that for Bosnia (serving with UNPROFOR from 1992). The design of this unnamed bronze medal is the same for each issue but there is a different coloured ribbon for each area of service. Since 1979 personnel who have

Left: The UN Service Medal for Cyprus, obverse, with the badge of the UN.

Below left: The UN Service Medal. Standard obverse of the current medals.

Left: The UN Service Medal. Standard reverse of the current medal. The medals are all the same in design, with only the ribbon colours indicating the area of service (in this case for Bosnia).

Far left: *The NATO Service Medal. Standard obverse, with badge of NATO. Clasp 'Former Yugoslavia' for service in former Yugoslavian provinces.*

Left: *The NATO Service Medal. Standard reverse, with clasp 'Kosovo'. As with the UN issues, the medal is the same in each case with clasps and ribbon colours indicating areas of service.*

served on more than one tour of duty wear on the appropriate ribbon a silver numeral denoting the number of tours.

The NATO Service Medal, 1994 to date

Events in the Balkans and the intervention of NATO forces resulted in the issuing of this medal in 1994. As with the UN awards, the medal is to be the same in each instance, thin bronze and unnamed, but with slide-on clasps and coloured ribbons to distinguish the area of service. Thirty days' service is required within the area of operation, or ninety days in support operations outside the actual area.

Several types have so far been awarded to British personnel. These

'Hearts and Minds': a British bandsman serving with the UN in the former Yugoslavia entertains local children.

The NATO medal with ribbon for service in Macedonia. Note that it does not carry a clasp – this is because of an ongoing international dispute over the actual status of Macedonia.

include the medal with ribbon and clasps *Former Yugoslavia* and *Kosovo* or simply with ribbon (not clasp) for *Macedonia*. All of these were for peace-keeping service in the Balkans in the wake of the terrible civil wars of the 1990s which devastated the region and led to the break-up of Yugoslavia.

Other clasps have also been issued to NATO forces. The medal with clasp *Article 5* has distinct ribbons for both operations 'Eagle Assist' (NATO air surveillance over the Balkans from 9th October 2001 to 16th May 2002) and 'Active Endeavour' (for naval service in the Mediterranean in support of NATO actions in the Balkans from 26th October 2001). The clasp *Non Article 5* is awarded for service in the Balkans after 3rd December 2002 and replaces the earlier *Former Yugoslavia* and *Kosovo* awards. The clasp *ISAF* (i.e. International Security Assistance Force) has been granted to NATO forces serving in Afghanistan.

It should be noted that it is not possible to receive the UN and the NATO medal for service in the same operations – British forces will be serving *either* as part of the UN or as part of NATO forces and will qualify for the appropriate award. Similarly, they would not be entitled to the ISAF award since there is a separate Operational Service Medal for Afghan operations (see page 39).

As with UN awards, those who have taken part in more than one operational tour wear a small numeral on the ribbon to denote the number of tours.

Mentions in Dispatches

t has long been the custom for senior officers to mention in official reports the names of officers and men who have rendered distinguished or gallant services but who are not necessarily recommended for a decoration. Only at the end of the First World War (which brought forward thousands of personnel worthy of some form of recognition) was there any emblem to show that a person had been so honoured. In 1919 it was decreed that personnel who had been mentioned would wear a bronze oakleaf spray on the ribbon of the appropriate campaign medal. For the First World War the emblem would be worn only on the ribbon of the Victory Medal. Later the emblem was altered to a single bronze oakleaf. For the Second World War this is worn only on the ribbon of the 1939–45 War Medal, not on that of a campaign star. Only one emblem is worn, irrespective of the number of times a person has been mentioned in a particular campaign. Since 1993, the emblem has been in silver.

Emblem of oakleaves, indicating a Mention in Dispatches prior to August 1920. For 1914–18 service, the emblem is worn on the Victory Medal ribbon.

Right: *Single oakleaf emblem, indicating a Mention in Dispatches after August 1920. Still current and worn (since 1993 in silver) on the ribbon of the appropriate campaign medal. For 1939–45 service, it is borne only on the ribbon of the War Medal.*

The 'Mention in Dispatches' oakleaf emblem in silver, as awarded after 1993. It is sewn on to the ribbon of the appropriate campaign medal.

Medal designers

Most British medals are designed by the resident engravers of the Royal Mint. Some of the obverses, which are officially approved images of the monarch, also feature on contemporary coins or stamps. Sometimes the designs (especially for the more varied reverses) are opened to competition and the designer's name or initials are frequently found on the reverse. Many of these designers were established artists, sculptors or medallists.

Africa General Service Medal reverse: G. W. de Saulles
India General Service Medal 1908–35 reverse: Richard Garbe
1914 Star and 1914–15 Star obverse: W. H. J. Blakemore
British War Medal reverse: W. McMillan
Mercantile Marine Medal reverse: Harold Stabler
Victory Medal reverse: W. McMillan
Naval General Service Medal reverse: Miss Margaret Winser
General Service Medal 1918 reverse: E. Carter Preston
India General Service Medal 1936 reverse: H. Wilson Parker
Defence Medal obverse: T. H. Paget
Defence Medal reverse: H. Wilson Parker
War Medal 1939–45 reverse: E. Carter Preston
Korean War Medal reverse: E. Carter Preston
Korean War Medal obverse: Mrs Mary Gillick CBE
        (also used on Africa General Service Medal, clasp *Kenya*)
General Service Medal 1962 reverse: T. H. Paget
South Atlantic Medal reverse: R. Lowe
Iraq Medal 2003 reverse: Major M. Atkinson

Unless listed above, designs on British issues should be taken as the work of the Royal Mint's artists.

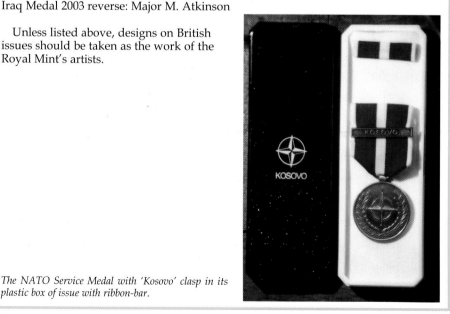

The NATO Service Medal with 'Kosovo' clasp in its plastic box of issue with ribbon-bar.

Following up

Anyone interested in collecting campaign medals should buy one or two basic reference books in addition to any unit or campaign histories which may be required. *British Battles and Medals* in its editions by Major L. L. Gordon or in its current version by Spink is an essential guide. Alec Purves's *Collecting Decorations and Medals* is useful, as are his *The Medals, Decorations and Orders of the Great War* and *The Medals, Decorations and Orders of World War Two* (Hayward, 1989 and 1986). Also recommended is the annual *Medals Yearbook* (Token Publishing). Militaria and medal collectors' magazines like *Medal News* (Token Publishing) or *The Armourer* (Beaumont Press) are useful sources of information and give details of dealers and fairs. Campaign medals of an earlier period, gallantry awards in general and Britain's most prestigious gallantry award in particular are dealt with respectively in three books by the present author in the same series: *British Campaign Medals 1815–1914* (Shire, 2000; reprinted 2004); *British Gallantry Awards 1855–2000* (Shire, 2001; reprinted 2005); and *The Victoria Cross* (Shire, 2005).

Libraries or information centres will have details of local medal or militaria collectors' societies. National societies should be considered: the Orders and Medals Research Society is the largest, but others are relevant – The Military Historical Society, The Indian Military Historical Society and The Orders and Medals Society of America may all be of interest. Each produces a periodic journal that can be a valuable source of information and contacts.

Important medal collections are held by the National Army Museum in Chelsea, the Imperial War Museum in Lambeth, London, and military museums around Britain. As there are about 150 regimental museums, most with fine collections of orders, decorations and campaign medals, the reader is advised to consult *A Guide to Military Museums* by T. and S. Wise (Imperial Press), which lists all the military museums, giving visitors' details and contact numbers.

Although it is still possible to find medals in antique shops or markets, such finds

A modern medal group, showing the Operational Service Medal for Sierra Leone, the NATO medal with ribbon and clasp 'Former Yugoslavia' and (right) the 2002 Jubilee Medal.

are becoming rarer. The serious collector will need to use the shops or postal lists of specialist dealers or the major auction houses dealing in medals. Regular militaria or medal fairs are held most weekends all round Britain and are well worth attending. Addresses, dates and contacts are to be found in collectors' magazines and journals.

Useful addresses

The Orders and Medals Research Society: Membership Secretary, OMRS, PO Box 1904, Southam, Warwickshire CV47 2ZX. Website: www.omrs.org.uk

The Military Historical Society: National Army Museum, Royal Hospital Road, London SW3 4HT. Telephone: 020 7730 0717.

The Indian Military Historical Society: Secretary, 33 High Street, Tilbrook, Huntingdon, Cambridgeshire PE28 0JP.

Some leading dealers

(These issue regular sales lists to subscribers and attend weekend fairs.)

Andrew Bostock, 15 Waller Close, Leek Wootton, Warwickshire CV35 7QG. Telephone/fax: 01926 856381. Website: www.bostockmedals.co.uk

Philip Burman, The Cottage, Blackborough End, Middleton, King's Lynn, Norfolk PE32 1SE. Telephone: 01553 840350. Website: www.military-medals.co.uk

Peter Cotrel, 7 Stanton Road, Bournemouth, Dorset BH10 5DS. Telephone/fax: 01202 388367; mobile: 07971 019155.

C. J. and A. J. Dixon, First Floor, 23 Prospect Street, Bridlington, East Yorkshire YO15 2AE. Telephone: 01262 603348 or 676877. Website: www.dixonsmedals.co.uk

Spink & Son, 69 Southampton Row, Bloomsbury, London WC1B 4ET. Telephone: 020 7563 4000. Website: www.spink-online.com

Auction houses

Bonhams (incorporating Glendining's), 101 New Bond Street, London W1S 1SR. Telephone: 020 7447 7447. Website: www.bonhams.com

Dix, Noonan, Webb, 16 Bolton Street, London W1J 5BQ. Telephone: 020 7016 1700. Website: www.dnw.co.uk

Morton & Eden, 45 Maddox Street, London W1S 2PE. Telephone: 020 7493 5344. Website: www.mortonandeden.com

Spink & Son, 69 Southampton Row, Bloomsbury, London WC1B 4ET. Telephone: 020 7563 4000. Website: www.spink-online.com